W9-AKD-635

SANDRA CISNEROS

Latina Writer and Activist

Caryn Mirriam-Goldberg

Enslow Publishers, Inc.
40 Industrial Road
Box 398
Berkeley Heights, NJ 07922
USA

PO Box 38
Aldershot
Hants GU12 6BP
UK

http://www.enslow.com

Library of Congress Cataloging-in-Publication Data

Mirriam-Goldberg, Caryn
Sandra Cisneros, Latina writer and activist / Caryn Mirriam-Goldberg.
p. cm. — (Hispanic biographies)
Includes bibliographical references and index.
Summary: Surveys the life and work of this award-winning Latina author.
ISBN 0-7660-1045-7
1. Cisneros, Sandra—Juvenile literature. 2. Women authors, American—20th century—Biography—Juvenile literature. 3. Mexican American authors—Biography—Juvenile literature. 4. Mexican American women—Biography—Juvenile literature. [1. Cisneros, Sandra. 2. Authors, American. 3. Mexican Americans—Biography. 4. Women—Biography.] I. Title. II. Series.
PS3553.I78Z77 1998
818'.5409—dc21
[b] 98-20828
CIP
AC

Printed in the United States of America

10 9 8 7 6 5 4 3 2

Illustration Credits: C. M. Hardt (*The New York Times*), p. 8; Recreated by Enslow Publishers, Inc., pp. 15, 69; © Corel Corporation, pp. 12, 59, 78; Eric M. Thor, pp. 19, 27, 29, 40, 45, 53; Courtesy of Carolyn S. Sheafer, pp. 33, 35; Analisa Lee, p. 42; Jason Winn, p. 64; Ralph Barrera, p. 84.

Cover Illustration: AP/Wide World Photos

Contents

The Girl With the Bad Report Cards

On a rainy winter afternoon, the writer Sandra Cisneros stands before a ragtag group of children and adults in the tiny Brownsville branch of the Brooklyn Public Library, and with orange and black cat-eyed glasses perched atop her head, begins the song of life in the barrio.[1]

On that day, Cisneros passed around her fifth-grade report cards. "I have *C*'s and *D*'s in everything. . . . The only *B* I had was in conduct," Cisneros said. "But I don't remember being that stupid."[2]

Clearly, Sandra Cisneros, whose books have been translated into many languages and whose writing has won many awards, is not stupid. But growing up Latina in a poor neighborhood on the South Side of Chicago, Sandra often found that her teachers did not [illegible] "They thought I was a [illegible] that the best she could achieve in her [illegible] married, have chil[illegible] supermarket. [illegible], Cisneros has [illegible] goals. Unmarried and nobody's mother, she supports herself by writing. [illegible] of short stories, [illegible] less articles and interviews.

Teacher thought she had no hope ~~and~~ because she lived in a poor neighborhood on the South side of chicago. page 6

Cisneros is "one of only a handful of Latina writers to make it big on the American scene," according to Mary B.W. Tabor, a reporter for *The New York Times*.[4] In fact, her last two books each won her six-figure advances, something almost unheard of for a Latina writer in the publishing industry. In addition, Cisneros has received some of the most prestigious honors awarded to writers. Since 1981, Cisneros has won three National Endowment for the Arts grants. Her first book of fiction, *The House on Mango Street*, won the Before Columbus American Book Award in 1985. Even more notable, she received the Lannan Literary

Award in 1991 as well as a MacArthur "Genius Grant" fellowship in 1995.

Sandra Cisneros has also earned the praise of many other writers and critics. Reporter Peter S. Prescott of *Newsweek* hails her as "an original—we haven't heard anything like it before,"[5] and a commentator for the *Washington Post Book Review* called her "a writer of power and eloquence and great lyrical beauty."[6] African-American novelist Bebe Moore Campbell wrote: "In a land where our views of Hispanic people are often limited or distorted, Sandra Cisneros offers precious glimpses of the internal workings of their lives. She is an educator, unerring and relentless; she is not only a gifted writer but an absolutely essential one."[7]

Cisneros's goal as a writer is not just to entertain or involve readers, but to motivate them to improve the world. "I have the power to make people think in a different way. It's a different way of defining power, and it is something that I don't want to abuse or lose," Cisneros explains. "I want to help my community."[8]

And that she does. In writing about a people often ignored in popular literature and in telling vital stories especially for women and girls, she reaches well beyond the barrio. She helps readers around the world see that there are many ways to be American, and many ways to be female. Most of all, she helps people in the Latino community see the value of their stories.

Sandra Cisneros enjoys speaking to groups of young people and encouraging them to follow their dreams.

Even with such praise and prizes, she does not forget the hard years growing up poor and being a lackluster student. She says that every time she is asked to sign a book, she feels like laughing. "It's so wacky," she explains. "I was the girl with the *C*'s and *D*'s. I was the girl in the corner with the goofy glasses from Sears. I was the ugly kid in the class with the bad haircut, the one nobody would talk to. I was the one that never got picked to be in the play."[9] Now she writes the books others have turned into plays. And she writes the books that kids everywhere read in school.

So Cisneros stands in front of classrooms, particularly in the Latino neighborhoods of many cities, and tries to help the kids think in a different way about their own future. Sandra Cisneros, who grew up without permission to dream big, is on a mission to give kids hope. "You have to give them permission to have a dream."[10]

Straddling Two Countries

Sandra Cisneros was born in Chicago, Illinois, but she was actually born into the traditions, histories, and languages of two countries: the United States and Mexico. Her father was Mexican, and her mother was Mexican American. Her family spoke two languages and frequently journeyed to Mexico for long visits with her father's family. Cisneros grew up straddling two countries, each with its own challenges and gifts, each with its own way of defining Mexicans, Americans, and Mexican Americans.

One of the most difficult aspects of being Mexican American, explains Cisneros, lies in the simple term used to refer to people who come from Spanish-speaking countries: *Hispanic*. A Hispanic is commonly defined as anyone who speaks Spanish as a first language or has an ancestor who did, thus lumping together Spaniards, Puerto Ricans, Mexicans, and even Americans with Spanish-speaking relatives. Cisneros says that when she grew up, everyone in her family referred to themselves as *Latino* or *Latina* (for females), a word encompassing people from Spanish-speaking countries in North and South America. Some Mexican Americans, including Cisneros herself, prefer to call themselves *Chicano* or *Chicana* (females), terms that refer specifically to Mexican Americans.

All of Sandra Cisneros's grandparents came from Mexico, and two of them never left. Her father's parents lived their whole lives in Mexico. But before her grandfather met and married his wife, he was a somewhat rebellious cadet in Mexico's military academy and had to flee and hide because "it was not fortunate to be a cadet during the Mexican revolution."[1] The Revolution of 1910 spawned bands of soldiers throughout the country that fought federal troops. The frequent warfare going on all around put any soldiers, and even soldiers-in-training such as Cisneros's grandfather, at great risk of getting hurt or killed. Instead of fighting on the front lines, he headed northeast to Philadelphia to get a taste of life in the United States. Although he returned to Mexico to begin his career and

Sandra Cisneros was born in Chicago.

his family, his taste of America was passed down to his three children, especially his son Alfredo.

Cisneros's grandfather eventually became a career military man and was often an absent father, who was too involved in the military to spend time with his family.[2] His first son and Cisneros's father, Alfredo Cisneros Del Moral, was born near Mexico City because that was where the army was stationed at the time. Alfredo's mother was the main parent for Alfredo and her two other children.

Alfredo and his siblings grew up in a very strict, military-style home with many of the privileges only afforded to members of the wealthy class like themselves. One of those privileges included going away to college. According to Cisneros, her father "spent that first year gambling, and going after ladies, and having a good time." When his grades were mailed home, Alfredo ran away rather than face his father. "My father was the favorite son in the family of five, and he ran away like a prodigal son. Out of terror," says Cisneros.[3]

Unlike Alfredo Cisneros's wealthy Mexican family, Cisneros's mother, Elvira Cordero Anguiano, grew up in poverty. Her parents came from Guanajuato, Mexico, where they lived a fairly common rural life. But the Mexican Revolution, which lasted until 1917, brought both the government officials and the revolutionaries to their land. To the common people, Cisneros explains, "It didn't matter what side you were on." Her mother's mother often told her both the government officials and the revolutionaries would "steal your chickens and rape your women."[4]

Eventually, to escape the danger of being in the cross fire between the revolutionaries and the government officials, and to make a better life for his family, Cisneros's maternal grandfather moved north with the railroad. He first worked in Flagstaff, Arizona, then in other cities until he saved enough money to send for his wife and her family, including her brothers and mother. Such a journey fits the typical pattern of Mexican immigration.

By the 1940s, Cisneros's mother's family had settled in Chicago. Cisneros's grandfather continued to work for the railroad while he and his wife raised their children in a poor Mexican neighborhood. There, Elvira and her siblings took on the ways and language of their new country and lost touch with their relatives in Mexico.

Meanwhile, Alfredo Cisneros Del Moral, who had come to the United States during World War II, soon found himself faced with an ultimatum. The government officials who picked him up as an illegal alien gave him the choice of being deported back to Mexico or joining the United States Army. So Alfredo Cisneros became a United States citizen and served in the Army, all without being able to speak English. "He used to have to ask the Puerto Ricans or any Spanish speakers in the Army what was going on," says Cisneros.[5]

The end of World War II led Alfredo Cisneros back to his "vagabonding" around America.[6] Now he traveled not as a tourist but as a United States citizen and World War II veteran. He also had the opportunity to travel with his brother who had moved to the United States a few years earlier. During one of their jaunts from New York to California, the combination of a bus stop, cold weather, and a quick decision to get off the bus for a break were to change the rest of Alfredo Cisneros's life. According to Sandra Cisneros, when the bus stopped in Chicago, her father said, "Well, I've

Sandra Cisneros's mother and father were born in Mexico and her family would often return there for extended visits.

heard there's lots of Mexicans here. Let's get off here for a little while."[7] He and his brother were to live in Chicago the rest of their lives.

Shortly after his arrival, Alfredo Cisneros met Elvira Cordero at a dance. Cisneros says her mother disliked her father at first because he came from a wealthy family and bragged about how much money he made. "She always said she couldn't stand him because he was such a show-off. I don't know why she married him," Cisneros jokes.[8]

However, she eventually came to love him, and soon they married, merging Elvira Cordero's poor immigrant family and Alfredo Cisneros's well-off Mexican family into Cisneros's family of origin.

Elvira Cisneros worked in a factory for a number of years while her husband, without the financial support of his family, found a way to make a living as an upholsterer. He also knew how to fix almost anything that went wrong with their apartment. The hard work took a toll on him, and years later, his daughter wrote a poem describing herself as the "Daughter of / a daddy with a hammer and blistered feet / he'd dip into a washtub while he ate his dinner."[9]

All that hard work was necessary to support his growing family. During the 1940s and 1950s, Elvira Cisneros gave birth to eight children—six sons and two daughters. The first two sons were followed by a daughter who died. But that sorrow was softened on

December 20, 1954, by the birth of a girl they named Sandra. And her last name, Cisneros, which means "keeper of swans," may have been fitting. Like the fabled ugly duckling, Sandra Cisneros did not appear elegant and graceful until she was grown.

By that time, the family lived in Humboldt Park, an area populated by Mexicans, Mexican Americans, and Puerto Ricans. The first language Cisneros, and the four brothers born after her, heard was Spanish, and one of their first foods was tamales. But the Cisneros kids also heard English and ate hamburgers.

"I grew up with a Chicana mother and a Mexican father, and we spoke English to her and Spanish to him."[10] Most people in Cisneros's neighborhood spoke and understood both languages. "I think that if you're bilingual, you're doubly rich," she now says. "You have two ways of looking at the world."[11]

The one language everyone understood was the language of poverty. Cisneros's parents could only earn a limited amount of money, not enough to provide all they wanted for the many children they had. The Cisneros family lived mostly in run-down apartment buildings. Often her parents would choose the top-floor apartment because they believed "noise travelled down" and "it was wiser to be the producer of noise rather than its victim."[12] The apartments where Cisneros lived, all on the west and northwest sides of Chicago where most Puerto Ricans, Mexicans, and other Spanish-speaking people lived, were often too small and infested with cockroaches and mice.

In fact, Cisneros developed a fear of mice because "to me mice are all my poverty, the whole neighborhood I grew up in, embodied in a little skittering creature that might come to get me at any moment. I don't ever want to live like that again. It's horrible."[13]

Money was in short supply for the Cisneros family, sometimes forcing them to move from apartment to apartment. The moves, each entailing a new neighborhood and new school, unsettled Cisneros and made her introverted and shy. Never one to make friends easily, each move made her feel more and more alone.[14]

Yet Cisneros also recalls a childhood full of people, sometimes too many in a small space. Neighborhood friends and the many relatives of her mother would stream through wherever they lived. And even when it was just the family at home, it was nine people trying to make do in a few rooms. She explains that her parents would have recalled her childhood as anything but lonely with everyone crammed into the apartment, "children sleeping on the living room couch and fold-out Lazy Boy, and on beds set up in the middle room, where the only place with any privacy was the bathroom."[15]

But if their apartments in Chicago were poor and crowded, the Mexican home of Alfredo Cisneros's

The crowded apartments that Sandra Cisneros lived in as a child were in poor neighborhoods.

family in Oaxaca was well-appointed and spacious. Cisneros's grandparents' house, on "numero 12" La Fortuna, was a warm and welcome retreat, especially in contrast to the fierce Chicago winters. Sandra and her brothers would play and visit with relatives there, completely immersed in Mexican culture.

The trips, says Cisneros, were motivated by her father's longing for the old country, and they caused the family enormous inconvenience and instability. Cisneros explains that trips to Mexico often meant the family would, "let go our flat, store the furniture with mother's relatives, load the station wagon with baggage and bologna sandwiches and head south."[16] Then, after days of driving in a cramped station wagon with her many brothers, they arrived at "that famous house, the only constant in the series of traumatic upheavals we experienced as children, and no doubt for a stubborn period of time, my father's only legitimate 'home' as well."[17] But eventually, after weeks visiting, it would be time to head north again. Alfredo and Elvira Cisneros viewed America as their real home.

"We came back, of course, to yet another Chicago flat, another Chicago neighborhood, another Catholic school," Cisneros says. Returning each time was depressing for the family "because we moved so much and always in neighborhoods that appeared like France after World War II—empty lots and burned-out buildings."[18]

In addition, the vacations in Mexico and regular life in Chicago left Cisneros feeling split between two cultures too far apart in too many ways. She often felt "almost like a foreigner," she explains, because "in some sense we're not Mexican and in some sense we're not American."[19] In Mexico, where she looked and sounded like a native, she was a visitor. In Chicago, outside her own neighborhood, she was a minority with an extra language and skin too dark to be seen as beautiful in American magazines or movies.

Years later, Cisneros saw how straddling two cultures actually enriched her life in many ways. As a child, though, she felt mostly like an outsider who did not really fit in anywhere. It was not until her school years, when she began reading and writing, that she found ways to bridge the distance between Mexico and America in herself.

Seven Fathers and One Strong-Willed Mother

"I am the only daughter in a family of six sons," says Sandra Cisneros. "*That* explains everything."[1] So because she was female, Cisneros had seven men telling her what she could and could not do. "So, in essence I feel like I grew up with seven fathers," she explains.[2] But Cisneros also grew up with a very strong-willed mother, one who enabled Cisneros to aim high and pursue her goals with faith and gusto. She credits this combination—seven fathers and one strong mother—with leading her into the writing life.

The men in her family, like many Mexican and Mexican-American men, believed they knew what was best for women. Her father, having grown up in a very traditional and strict Mexican household, "believed daughters were meant for husbands."[3] He wanted his daughter to grow up, marry, and have children just as his mother and his wife had done. "I guess as Mexican daughters we're not supposed to have our own house. We have our father's house and then he hands us over to our husband's," Cisneros explains.[4]

Being a girl also made her invisible at times to her brothers and father. Her older brothers soon paired off, as did the two brothers born after her, and the twin boys born after them. "These three sets of men had their own conspiracies and allegiances, leaving me odd-woman-out forever," Cisneros writes. Her brothers ". . . all kind of teamed up and excluded me from their games."[5] Being the only girl made her feel shy and ignored.

Her father's attitude added to her isolation. She tells the story of how, each time they moved to another Chicago neighborhood, her father would pull aside the parish priest of the Catholic school to ask for a tuition discount. Then he would either complain or boast, "I have seven sons." He would repeat the same statement to people constantly, she recalls, to anyone he met: "The Sears Roebuck employee who sold us the washing machine. The short-order cook where my father ate his ham-and-eggs breakfasts. . . . As if he deserved a medal from the state." And always she would tug his sleeve and whisper: "'Not seven sons. Six! and *one daughter*.'"[6]

So Sandra Cisneros grew up "the only daughter and *only* a daughter," as she wrote in a note for an anthology that contained her writing. Years later when she thought about writing that statement, she realized that she could have written several statements to describe her childhood, including, "I am the only daughter of a Mexican father and a Mexican-American mother" or "I am the only daughter of a working-class family of nine." She explains, "all of these had everything to do with who I am today."[7] But being the only daughter also had advantages.

Cisneros now says she is lucky that her father and brothers thought girls were meant only to be wives and that her brothers were too busy to spend time with her. It forced her to spend time alone since her brothers "felt it was beneath them to play with a *girl* in public. But that aloneness, that loneliness, was good for a would-be writer—it allowed me time to think and think, to imagine, to read and prepare myself."[8] It was not the men in her family, however, that truly encouraged her to pursue her interests. Her strong-willed mother played an essential role.

Her mother was always a woman guided by a strong will, one who, as a girl, would sneak out the window to play after being put to bed. Cisneros says her mother "rejected her own mother as a role model and instead, adopted the cynicism, the independence, and the eccentricity of her [Elvira's] father."[9] After all, Elvira's father was the one who, years before, brought his entire family over a thousand miles north to live a new and unknown life in America. Some of that daring, Cisneros believed, passed on to Elvira Cordero.

Such an upbringing resulted in her being determined that her daughter pursue her dreams rather than conform to a life of cooking and cleaning for men. "She had to be a woman like that in order to raise me in the wicked way that she did, because she didn't make me conform to models that were given to her."[10] Cisneros credits her mother: "I'm the product of a fierce woman who was brave enough to raise her daughter in a nontraditional way," even fighting for Cisneros to develop into a writer.[11] Her mother routinely excused her from housework so Sandra could read and write. So Cisneros grew up being granted the time, space, and support to study, read, and write. Elvira clearly did not want her only daughter to be "only a daughter."

School added to this "only daughter's" isolation. Cisneros attended Catholic schools in Chicago, calling her basic education "rather shabby."[12] After starting kindergarten in 1959, Sandra was to attend one Catholic school after another, occasionally disappearing for weeks to go to Mexico with her family. With so many students from Mexico attending these schools, school officials knew how to make adjustments along the way.

Early on, she was enrolled at St. Callistus, which she describes as very racist. She explains that the Italian kids dominated the schools and Latinos like herself were the minority. Furthermore, the nuns, whom she described as cruel, "were majestic at making one feel little."[13] Because she did not want the nuns to make fun of or belittle her, Sandra hid her desire to write. Girls, and especially poor Mexican-American girls, were not supposed to read, write, and study so much. Girls were expected to go to school, perhaps even graduate, but then marry and have children, working outside the home in menial jobs whenever extra income was needed. Returning to her neighborhood years later, Cisneros told Chicago school kids, "In all the schools I went to, nobody told me I could be writer, but I just kept on writing."

At home she often had to share a bedroom with noisy brothers, and a small apartment with the many people of her immediate family. She remembers longing for a home of her family's own throughout her childhood. What this only daughter wanted most of all she finally got, but not in the way she had wished. It was not until Cisneros was twelve years old that her parents borrowed enough money to make a down payment on a small, ugly two-story bungalow in one of Chicago's Puerto Rican neighborhoods. Although it

Sandra Cisneros does not have pleasant memories of her early schooling at St. Callistus.

was a house, it was also a house so small, crooked, and crowded that Sandra was more ashamed than pleased with the new home.

However, the first real house Sandra could call home, on the 1500 block of North Campbell Avenue in Chicago, did afford her a bedroom of her own. She was the only person in her family to have her own room, "a narrow closet just big enough for my twin bed and an oversized blond dresser we'd bought in the bargain basement of *el Sears*." But the dresser, "long as a coffin" prevented her from "the luxury of shutting the door."[14]

A room of her own at least gave her more opportunities to read and write, and a new school enhanced those opportunities. After transferring to St. Aloysius, run by the Sisters of Christian Charity, she found support for her love of books. "They recognized that I was doing all this reading outside of class and that I was smart," she says. They encouraged her to read more and more.

As a result of such a solitary upbringing, which included moving too much to make long-term friends and growing up the only daughter, Sandra's interest in books was intense. "Had my sister lived or had we stayed in one neighborhood long enough for a friendship to be established, I might not have needed to bury myself in books the way I did," Cisneros writes. "I remember, I especially like reading about 'the olden times' because the past seemed more interesting than

The first home that the Cisneros family owned was a small bungalow similar to the ones pictured here.

my dull present." Books magically changed her surroundings into "something wonderful."[15]

She did not find many books in her home. On the contrary, her family owned only two books: a Bible her mother bought with S & H Green Stamps (coupons given out by supermarkets that could be exchanged for household items) and a worn copy of *Alice in Wonderland* found in the bargain basement of a Sears department store. But she turned to books anyway, in large part because her school required students to take books out of the class library. "Since our school was poor, so were the choices," Cisneros laments.[16] The result, she said, was reading many books that she might not have chosen on her own: She enjoyed 1890s, Horatio Alger–type tales (rags-to-riches stories about a young man) and books on the lives of the Catholic saints.

She soon moved on to what she called the most important books of her childhood, which included several fairy tales. Not surprisingly, she loved Hans Christian Andersen's "Six Swans," the story of an only sister like herself who helped her brothers, who had been bewitched into swans, become human again. She read the tale again and again, years later asking, "Was it not coincidence my family name [Cisneros] translated 'keeper of swans'?" Besides dreaming herself the sister in "Six Swans," she dreamed herself Andersen's ugly duckling. That duckling was "ridiculous, ugly, perennially the new kid. But one day the spell would wear off."[17]

But the tale she read the most was Virginia Lee Burton's *The Little House*, a picture book. *The Little House* tells the story of a beloved house whose owner promises never to sell it. But after many years, the house is abandoned and falls apart. Luckily, the great granddaughter of the house's builder rescues the house. The house appealed to Cisneros and still does because of its permanence and order. "Wasn't *The Little House* the house I dreamed of, a house where one family lived and didn't move away?" she asks. "One house, one spot." She read and reread the book, and even schemed with a brother to steal it. They planned to say they had lost the book, and then it would be theirs forever. "That was the plan, a good one, but never executed—good, guilty Catholics that we were."[18]

Strangely enough, Sandra did not know that one could buy a book at a bookstore until years later. "For a long time I believed they were so valuable as to only be dispensed to institutions and libraries, the only place I'd seen them."[19]

The books fed the undeveloped writer within her. "I was reading and reading, nurturing myself with books like vitamins, only I didn't know it then," she says.[20] The stories Sandra read took root even after she put the book down, and she found that the more she read, the more she began to write in her head. Even at a young age, she composed stories in her head, sometimes creating them out of the events of her daily life. Cisneros gives an example of how a voice in her head began narrating the ordinary events of her life:

> I want you to go to the store and get me a loaf of bread and a gallon of milk. Bring back all the change and don't let them gyp you like they did last time." In my head the narrator would add: . . . *she said in a voice that was neither reproachful nor tender. Thus clutching the coins in her pocket, our hero was off under a sky so blue and a wind so sweet she wondered it didn't make her*

> *dizzy*. This is how I glamorized my days living in the third-floor flats and shabby neighborhoods where the best friend I was always waiting for never materialized.[21]

By the time she began Josephium High School in 1968 she was waiting less and writing more. At a time when other girls were dating, she was still a self-described ugly duckling attending an all-girls school. Had there been any boys interested in her, "I would have thrown myself into love the way some warriors throw themselves into fighting. I was ready to sacrifice everything in the name of love, to do anything, even risk my own life." As a young girl who had "enough imagination to fall in love all by myself," Cisneros sees now how her life could have taken a completely different route if she had met a boy then who had wanted her.[22]

Sandra began to show her creativity to others more. She began to read poems in class, and by her sophomore year, she met a teacher who loved writing and wanted to be a writer. The teacher encouraged Sandra to write more, and even to work on the school literary magazine. Eventually she became the editor of the literary magazine and saw some of her poetry published in it.

Although she had written throughout her four years in high school, enough so that all her classmates considered her to be the class poet, and she had served as editor of the literary magazine, she did not call herself

Sandra Cisneros began to write more seriously as a student at Josephium High School. Pictured are her freshman (left) and senior (right) yearbook pictures.

a writer then. "I was more a reader than a writer—an important first step to *becoming* a writer."[23] She was also noticing all kinds of details of her life and of her family, details she would draw from for stories and poems her whole life.

But Sandra Cisneros knew, even in high school, that she would write these stories and poems, although she could not say at what moment in her life that knowledge came:

> I don't know when I first said to myself I am going to be a writer. Perhaps that first day my mother took me to the public library when I was five, or perhaps again when I was in high school and my English teacher forced me to read a poem out loud and I became entranced with the sounds, or perhaps when I enrolled in that creative writing class in college, not knowing it would lead to other creative writing workshops and graduate school. Perhaps.[24]

As she wrote about the dreams of her neighborhood and family, she also began to realize her own dream of becoming a writer, not just of her people but for her people. As "the first woman in my family to pick up a pen and record what I see around me, a woman who has the power to speak and is privileged enough to be heard," Cisneros recognized early on that she had a responsibility to her community.[25] That responsibility included both recording what was and what could be, how people around her lived and how they

Sandra Cisneros (top, left) served as editor of her high school's literary magazine.

should live. "I felt, as a teenager, that I could not inherit my culture intact without revising some parts of it," she says.[26]

But to truly fulfill her desire to write and her sense of responsibility for her community, she needed more than her 1972 high school diploma. She needed to go to college.

A Yellow Weed Among the Hothouse Flowers

Sandra Cisneros's decision to attend college was both early and unusual for a poor Chicana girl. Having little money for essentials in her family, let alone extra luxuries like college, and being the only girl among six brothers, schooling beyond high school was a pipe dream for Cisneros. But it was a dream she went after with gusto. She remembers telling her father when she was only in fifth grade that she had plans to go to college: "I was sure he understood. I remember my father saying, '*Que bueno, mi'ja*, that's good.' That meant a lot to me, especially since my brothers thought the idea hilarious."[1] She did not realize her father favored the idea of college because he thought she would find a good husband there.

To Alfredo Cisneros Del Moral, college meant his daughter would find a man with a good job to marry. Looking back, Cisneros writes, "I'm lucky my father believed daughters were meant for husbands. It meant it didn't matter if I majored in something silly like English."[2] With her freedom to explore "something silly like English," Cisneros went on not to one college, but to two universities: Loyola University in Chicago and the University of Iowa, where she participated in one of the most prestigious creative writing programs in the country. The scholarships she earned paved the way. She studied poetry and fiction writing. Along the way, she learned why she needed to be a writer and speak for those who did not have the chance to attend college or write books.

Cisneros enrolled at Loyola University in Chicago in the fall of 1972. As one of the few people of color on campus, she immediately stood out. Her classmates assumed she was Puerto Rican or Mexican, she says, and many female students told her she looked exotic.[3] After a while they accepted her as a typical student, reading literature and writing papers. But most of the literature she read was written by white men. And even as she filled notebooks with her own writing, she did not encounter a single Chicano author. In fact, she was the only Mexican American majoring in English at Loyola University.

By her junior year in 1974, she was ready to take a bold step with her writing. She enrolled in a writing workshop where she would share her writing with classmates on a weekly basis, listen to their critiques, and hear how her poems and stories sounded when she read them aloud to an audience. Years later, she would credit this class with pushing her to declare herself a writer.

Once she got a taste of how much her writing improved in a workshop environment, Cisneros wanted to immerse herself in a more serious writing program where she could learn from other writers. At the same time, she was entranced with poets such as Donald Justice, James Wright, Marvin Bell, and Mark Strand, some of whom taught at the University of Iowa Writers' Workshop.

It seemed impossible for a poor Chicana girl from Chicago to attend the most prestigious creative writing program in the country. But with the help of one of her Loyola teachers who saw her talent, Cisneros applied during her senior year to Iowa's poetry program. On the merits of her talent and hard work, she was accepted for the 1976 fall semester. She would move away from home for the first time and, with a bachelor's degree in hand, would study for a Master of Fine Arts degree in creative writing.

A scholarship enabled Sandra Cisneros to attend Loyola University in Chicago.

Cisneros hoped to study with poets Donald Justice and Marvin Bell. When she arrived, she discovered they were both on sabbatical leave, time faculty members sometimes take off to work on their own writing and research. She also discovered what it felt like to be completely different from her fellow students. During her early days at the University of Iowa Writers' Workshop, she felt very lonely and different from her more wealthy and almost all-white classmates. Iowa, even in the progressive college town of Iowa City, has a relatively small population of people of color, especially compared with Cisneros's hometown of Chicago. She could not forget that she grew up in a working-class neighborhood "complete with drunken bums, families sleeping on crowded floors, and rats."[4]

This personal difficulty was compounded by the program itself, which Cisneros admits "was terribly cruel to her as well as to many of the other first-year students."[5] There was competition, tremendous pressure to produce great writing, and additional pressure to make lasting connections with prominent writers. The competitive atmosphere took its toll on many of the students, who focused on their own work and not on helping each other. "It didn't take me long to learn—after a few days being there—that nobody cared to hear what I had to say and no one listened to me even when I did speak," Cisneros remembers. "I became very frightened and terrified that first year."[6]

A turning point occurred for Cisneros one day when her class was discussing Gaston Bachelard's *The Poetics of Space*. Bachelard's book speaks of houses as literary symbols of people's inner selves. Cisneros soon realized that all her classmates, having grown up in houses, understood the symbol. Cisneros, who had longed her whole childhood for a real house, found the idea of saying a house symbolized the human soul offensive. "My house was a prison for me; I don't want to talk about [my] house."[7] She felt even more like a foreigner, having moved to Iowa from a house she was ashamed of "because if they saw that house they would equate the house with me and my value."[8] Although her family wanted a better house, "the best they could do was offer the miserable bungalow I was embarrassed with all my life."[9]

Her white, middle-class, and wealthy classmates all shared a history that did not include poverty and darker skin. Even if they acted polite, Cisneros felt different and out of place. Suddenly, Cisneros began to question herself as a writer. If everyone grew up in

Sandra Cisneros participated in one of the most prestigious creative writing programs in the country at the University of Iowa in Iowa City.

houses that symbolized their souls, and if her house only embarrassed her, then how could she fit in as a real writer? "My classmates were from the best schools in the country. They had been bred as fine hothouse flowers. I was a yellow weed among the city's cracks."[10]

Although this incident hurt her, it also made her realize that some of her power as a writer lay in her difference. "It was not until this moment when I separated myself, when I considered myself truly distinct, that my writing acquired a voice," she writes. "I knew I was a Mexican woman. But, I didn't think it had anything to do with why I felt so much imbalance in my life, whereas it had everything to do with it!"[11]

From this incident, Cisneros learned that she felt different because she was different. However, it also meant that she could write about something her classmates knew nothing about.[12] She credits this moment as a turning point for her whole career. "It had been as if all of the sudden I realized, 'Oh, my God! Here's something [poverty] that my classmates can't write about, and I'm going to tell you because I'm the authority on this—I can tell you.'"[13]

She could write about being a Mexican-American woman in the world. She could write about what gifts and challenges came her way because of who she was, where she grew up, and what she had as well as did not have in her life because she was not white, middle class, or male. "What did I know except third-floor flats?" she asks. "Surely my classmates knew nothing about that. That's precisely what I chose to write: about third-floor flats, and fear of rats, and drunk husbands [in the neighborhood] sending rocks through windows, anything as far from the poetic as possible."[14] From writing what she knew, she discovered the unique voice she had been unconsciously suppressing.

So Cisneros began to write what she lived and what others around her lived, including growing up as a shy Latina who moved back and forth from Mexico to Chicago, from apartment to apartment and school to school. She wrote poems like "Roosevelt Road" in the summer of 1977 about the poverty and embarrassment she lived with as a child. Moreover, she explores some of the dangers of living in such poverty:

> Mama said don't play in alleys
> because that's where dogs get rabies and
> bad girls babies
> Drunks carried knives
> but if you asked
> they'd give you money.[15]

Despite the dangers, there were treasures: a dollar bill found, and even morning glories climbing the stone walls.

The simple language and vivid descriptions of where she lived enabled her to speak to and for millions of others who also grew up not knowing what

Sandra Cisneros felt out of place among the wealthy students in her classes at the University of Iowa because they had not grown up in "third-floor flats" similar to the one pictured here.

having a house meant. But those she spoke for did experience surprising acts of kindness from the drunks in the neighborhood or the fragile beauty of morning glories climbing the walls of run-down buildings.

By and large, she began to write the types of stories that she wanted to read—stories about people she knew and cared about all her life. She also found a few students who, like herself, did not completely fit in and who also wrote similar stories; writers who were also not white or from well-off families. Some of those who encouraged her were teachers; others were fellow students that she knew.

One of the friends for life she made was Joy Harjo, an American Indian from Oklahoma who also felt lonely and out of place at the workshop. Harjo is famous today as one of the foremost American Indian poets. However, while she was in Iowa, Harjo and Cisneros gave each other support through difficult times. Harjo, a Creek Indian, wrote about growing up on a southwestern reservation; Cisneros, a Chicana, wrote about growing up in a Chicago barrio. Both understood what it meant to be considered an outsider by people around them.

Cisneros also found solace in what she read, especially as she moved beyond fairy tales and famous American, white, male authors. During her time in Iowa, she discovered many other writers of color, including Chinese-American novelist Maxine Hong Kingston, Chicano poet Gary Soto, and African-American novelist Toni Morrison. All were writing about the American experience of people who were labeled a *minority*.

In the midst of this exciting time of meeting and working with all kinds of poets and fiction writers, and living far from home in what surely felt like a foreign country, Sandra Cisneros began writing sketches about growing up female in the barrio. Although she probably did not know it at the time, the short vignettes of life she captured in these sketches were to form the manuscript of *The House on Mango Street*. This was Cisneros's first book, begun in 1978 and not published until 1984. The book took her back to the barrio and eventually enabled her to travel the world and, years later, to buy her own house. It also marked the blooming of the yellow weed into an enduring writer.

Back to the Barrio

After graduating from the University of Iowa Writers' Workshop in May 1978, Cisneros went back to the barrio. At twenty-four years of age, she brought with her a desire to share with other Latinos some of the confidence and direction she gained as a student and writer. With her she carried the beginnings of *The House on Mango Street* and a bevy of poems and stories to share at Chicago readings over the next five years. It was a time of reuniting with her family and her community, and it was a time of readying herself to move out into the world as a writer.

Cisneros wanted to teach, but even with an M.F.A. from a famous writing school, she had not considered applying for a university job. Later, she said her decision reflected a lack of faith in herself as a woman and a Latina. "Why? Because as women, we think we're not good enough, we have nothing to share at the university."[1] She adds that too many Latino people were led to believe they are not smart enough or good enough by movies and television shows that portrayed Spanish-speaking people as stupid or lazy.[2] She felt this way despite her mother's attempts to help her believe enough in herself.

In the summer of 1978, she accepted a job at the Latino Youth Alternative High School in Chicago, where she counseled teens who did not fit in at conventional high schools. Many of the youths she assisted were high school dropouts who did not believe they were smart enough or good enough to offer much to the world. Her students were often pregnant or had young children, or they had histories of drug or alcohol abuse, or crime. Some had learning disabilities or traumatic family situations. Her job at the school was as much social worker as counselor.

While she helped her students get their diplomas and search for jobs, they helped her write about Chicago street life. "When I was working with high school drop-outs in Chicago after graduate school, I was especially intrigued by what they said because they had a very poetic way of expressing themselves," she explains. "So at that point, I was like a linguist roaming around listening to people. Sometimes I was more concerned with the *how* than the *what* of what they said."[3]

Although her work at the high school drained her of creative energy, she still spent whatever time she had left writing. And she began taking her writing to the streets—and even below the streets. Her poetry readings in local coffeehouses caught the attention of the Chicago Transit Authority's new poetry project. The transit authority was printing poems on posters and displaying them alongside advertisements in buses and subways throughout the city. The Poetry Society of America, sponsoring the project for the transit authority, chose the poetry of Cisneros and of prominent writers such as Gwendolyn Brooks, Carl Sandburg, Ogden Nash, and others. Soon thousands of area commuters were reading the words of Sandra Cisneros, one of the few local writers featured.

The recognition helped her meet Gary Soto, one of the best known Mexican-American writers in the country. In turn, he helped her get her first book published. *Bad Boys*, a chapbook (a small book of poetry, usually twenty or fewer pages long) containing seven poems, was printed by Mango Press of San Jose, California. All the poems created a picture of some aspect of life in the barrio.

Cisneros delighted in having the chapbook published, and she relished her rewarding and challenging job. But poetry readings in coffeehouses and school auditoriums ate away at her writing time. She started turning down opportunities to speak or read in order to spend more time writing. And in early 1980, she took a slightly less demanding job at Loyola University, returning to work at the place where she was once a student. Now Cisneros worked as an administrative assistant who recruited students from local high schools. Since she was comfortable in the poorer neighborhoods in the city, she often made presentations at high schools that were populated by low-income and minority students. The students she encountered often felt comfortable enough with her to make her their counselor and confidant because Cisneros was Latina and she, too, grew up in low-income neighborhoods.

Sometimes Cisneros's job seemed overwhelming and hopeless. Many of the young people she visited had little chance of ever attending college or leaving the barrio. But the time she spent visiting one high school after another brought her a greater sense of purpose as a writer: "From this experience of listening to young Latinos whose problems were so great, I felt helpless; I was moved to do something to change their lives, ours, mine. I did the only thing I knew how."[4] She also drew from her family and from her own life. And as she wrote of her people, she also wrote in their language—a mixture of Spanish and English.

Trying to support herself and write at the same time was extremely difficult. She started to feel frustrated and trapped, unable to write the stories she needed to tell and unsure where telling them would lead. At the same time, she discovered that the poetic stories she was writing about growing up fit together in a pattern, showing a whole story. This story would become *The House on Mango Street*, a book actually, that needed her full attention as she edited and shaped the stories into a novel.

The book might never have been published had not two lucky things happened: The National Endowment for the Arts (NEA) gave Cisneros a grant to work on her writing, and an editor expressed deep interest in publishing the book. According to Cisneros, "the NEA grant arrived to save me,"[5] giving her enough money to live on for a year or so. And editor Nick Kanellos of *Revista Chicano-Riquena*/Arte Publico Press gave her the much-needed encouragement to develop her writing. She had met Kanellos, the editor of a small press and literary magazine that published Latino writers, when she submitted "Chanclas" (a short story) for a children's literature issue. He asked her to send any others if she had them. In fact, he wanted to publish an entire book of her work.

For Cisneros, the combination of the NEA grant and the request for a manuscript was too tempting to pass up. Already involved in a job and several local literary projects, she decided that if she was ever to have

In 1978, Sandra Cisneros counseled teenagers at the Latino Youth Alternative High School who were having problems at conventional high schools.

enough time to devote to her writing, she needed to leave the steady job, community work, and even Chicago itself with its many distractions of family and friends. And the money from the grant would allow her to do just that, but first she had six months left to finish out her job and two literary projects.

Eventually, in 1981, Sandra Cisneros escaped to Provincetown, Massachusetts, to work full time on *The House on Mango Street* and to hang out with her "best buddy from Iowa days," a fiction writer named

Dennis Mathis. Mathis served as her editor for what she feels are "the cleanest pieces in the book. Ultimately, I was writing to reach his standards."[6]

Each of the pieces tells of the bittersweet life in a Chicago barrio. While each chapter works as a story on its own, each is also part of the larger story. This structure, according to Cisneros, was not an accident. She wanted to write a book that a reader could pick up, open to any chapter, and find a story that made its own sense. "You would understand each story like a little pearl, or you could look at the whole thing like a necklace," says Cisneros. "That's what I always knew from the day that I wrote the first one. I said, 'I'm going to do a whole series of these, and it's going to be like this, and it'll all be connected.'"[7]

She succeeded in creating both pearls and a necklace linking them, but she did more than that. She told a story of a girl similar to herself, named Esperanza, who found herself becoming an artist to escape "the trap of the barrio."[8] Cisneros wanted to show people what life in the barrio was like as well as what it was not like. The book stood in sharp contrast to "those people who want to make our barrios look like Sesame Street, or some place really warm and beautiful," Cisneros says.[9] At a time when homes like the one she grew up in were either portrayed as "warm and beautiful" or ignored, Cisneros portrayed how poverty weighs people down, and how people may triumph anyway. She explains, "It's nice to go visit a poor neighborhood, but if you've got to live there every day, and deal with garbage that doesn't get picked up, and kids getting shot in your backyard, and people running through your gangway at night, and rats, and poor housing. . . . It loses its charm real quick!"[10]

Esperanza, a girl who believes in and hopes for a better life in *The House on Mango Street*, lives the everyday challenges of being poor and Mexican. But through her name, she helps readers see the hope buried under the trash and danger: "In English my name means hope," Esperanza says. "In Spanish it means too many letters. It means sadness, it means waiting. It is like the number nine. A muddy color. It is the Mexican records my father plays on Sunday mornings when he is shaving, songs like sobbing."[11] Esperanza leads readers through the barrio, always dreaming of a real house, one with stairs, several bathrooms, and a big yard full of trees and grass. She hopes, just like Cisneros hoped, for a house so "we don't have to pay rent to anybody, or share the yard with the people downstairs, or be careful not to make too much noise, and there isn't a landlord banging on the ceiling with a broom."[12]

Eventually both the fictional Esperanza and the real Cisneros find a home in their own hearts. And they make a promise to return and speak for the family and friends in the barrio they left behind.[13]

Borderland Blessings, Borderland Blues

The publication in 1984 of *The House on Mango Street* changed Sandra Cisneros's life in all ways and set in motion a writing career marked by critical acclaim, awards, and opportunities. One of those opportunities would land her in the border town of San Antonio, Texas, which would become her permanent home. But the success the book brought would not yet eliminate Cisneros's struggle to earn a living and maintain enough time to write.

Begun in 1977 in the cornfields of Iowa and written mostly in Chicago during the years 1979 to 1981, and in Massachusetts later in 1981, Cisneros finished

The House on Mango Street in 1982 on a Greek island, still living off the NEA grant of 1981. She recalls finishing the book at 4 A.M. on the day of her second deadline, after having missed the first deadline because she was not yet done with the revisions. Because she had been mailing the chapters to her publisher as she wrote them, she was never sure what she was creating at the time. Two days after she sent off the final chapters, she wrote to a friend, ". . . and now there is the terror of having to live with *Mango Street*. Like it or not, it is permanent and I will have to live with its permanent imperfections."[1] She would have almost two years of revisions, however, until the book came out in print in 1984.

In the meantime, she learned more about the people and places of other countries. During the spring of 1983, Cisneros served as artist-in-residence at the Michael Karolyi Foundation in Venice, Italy. An artist-in-residence program often allows writers and artists to work a certain number of hours each week, teaching classes about their writing or art, and to work the remainder of the time on their artistic projects. In Venice, Cisneros wrote more poems for her collection *My Wicked, Wicked Ways*, which was published by Third Woman Press in 1987.

Then, Cisneros settled down in Yugoslavia with a Yugoslavian boyfriend. "That was the summer I spent being a wife," explained Cisneros years later. And because Yugoslavia was still a Communist country with few available niceties such as toilet paper and coffee, she had to get used to living without many modern conveniences and even electricity at times. "I washed shirts by hand; with a broom and bucket of suds I scrubbed the tiles of the garden each morning from all the pigeon droppings that fell from the flock that lived on the roof of the garden shed."[2]

Although the relationship with her boyfriend did not last, she made a friend who did. Jasna K., a neighbor, met her one day as she sat on a wooden bench outside the summer kitchen of a garden shared by the two of them. "You looked at me as if you'd always known me, and I looked at you as if I'd always known you. Of that we were convinced," Cisneros wrote of their first meeting.[3] After that meeting, she visited Jasna frequently, helping her with the wash and other chores. Jasna, who had divorced her husband, lived with her mother and sister in an old stone house, and according to Cisneros, smoked too many cigarettes and was somewhat moody.[4]

They traded what they had and what they knew. "Remember the afternoons of kaffa (coffee), roasted in the garden, served in thimble-sized cups, the Turkish way?" Cisneros later wrote to Jasna.[5] Cisneros made Jasna a piñata (a paper animal stuffed with candy, very common at Mexican celebrations) for her

Sandra Cisneros was saddened to leave her friend Jasna behind in the war-torn country formerly known as Yugoslavia.

birthday and "joked it was the only piñata to be had in all of Yugoslavia."[6]

Cisneros realized that it was women like Jasna, whom she had befriended throughout Europe, that offered their encouragement and support without expecting something in return. When she was lost or alone, Cisneros would turn to Jasna and the others she had met to make her feel loved and cared for. And along the way, the women exchanged the stories of their lives, and Cisneros created several friendships that "crossed borders. It was like we all came from the same country, the women; we all had the same problems."[7] Those problems included, most of all, finding the right men to date and ways to support themselves while doing their art and writing.

Her friendship with Jasna, however, would stand out as an important connection in Cisneros's life. It would continue long after Cisneros returned to the United States. Jasna would even visit the United States to begin translating Cisneros's stories into Serbo-Croatian. But the friendship would also weigh heavy on Cisneros's heart years later when a divided Yugoslavia would bring years of war and devastation to Jasna's town.

Cisneros returned to the United States to write poetry and await early reviews of *The House on Mango Street*. She was pleased to discover that many reviewers thought the novel was poetic and very touching.

But it was more than the poetry of the writing that critics praised. Many saw in the book a strong political message. Cisneros communicates much of the confusion and complexities growing up Latina, Spanish-speaking, and low-income. Cisneros herself calls the book, "a very political work. It's really a book about a woman in her twenties coming to her political consciousness as a feminist woman of color."[8]

Cisneros wrote as a woman, as a Mexican American, and as a speaker of both Spanish and English in an English-speaking country. In doing so, she produced a novel that bridged several cultures. The book brings to many non-Latino classrooms the first real exposure to what it means to grow up Mexican American, what it means to grow up speaking Spanish, what it means to grow up poor, and what it means to grow up in all these ways as a woman.

Breaking barriers, Cisneros spoke of experiences common to many. This contributed to the book's adoption into junior and senior high school English classes all over America. Students in college and graduate school also began to read and study the novel in a variety of classes, including Chicano studies, psychology, creative writing, sociology, English, women's studies, and even sex education.

Cisneros may have been surprised because the money that this success brought her paid the bills for only a short time. But if that success did not bring her lasting financial security, it did take her places she had never been to before. After winning the impressive Before Columbus Award (an award given to an outstanding book by or about a minority) for *The House on Mango Street*, Cisneros received a job that took her to San Antonio, Texas, in 1984. Her new job was as an arts administrator at the Guadalupe Arts Center.

Once she arrived in Texas, she found that the mixed barrio of Mexicans, Mexican Americans, and other Latin Americans there had created a strong sense of community among those who spoke Spanish. She also found that she wanted to contribute to this community, and she soon became involved in organizing events to highlight the arts produced by the Chicano community.

As the organizer of the first small press book fair in the barrio, she brought together many Latino writers, publishers, and readers to celebrate their stories. Organizing the book fair took a tremendous amount of time and effort, and to Cisneros's disappointment, it drew mostly neighborhood people. While she was glad to see people from the neighborhood, she was disappointed that people outside that neighborhood did not attend the fair. After years of reading and attending readings and fairs for prominent white writers, she was angry that "white people never came to the neighborhood where I worked. I wasn't about to go into their neighborhood and start telling them about Chicano art."[9] While she still felt alienated at times from the people beyond the barrio, she began to find a real home for herself in this Texas barrio.

San Antonio, a border town that has grown into a city that supports the arts, represented the perfect balance for Cisneros. Having grown up traveling back and forth from Chicago to Mexico, she always felt split between two places. In San Antonio, however, she felt completely at home, still living in the United States but also living close to Mexico. "To me, it's exciting to be living in San Antonio, because to me it's the closest I can get to living in Mexico and still get paid," she says. "To me, San Antonio is where Latin America begins, and I love it. It's so rich."[10]

In her article "The Tejano Soul of San Antonio," published in *Texas Magazine* after Cisneros had lived in the city long enough to consider herself a native, she describes this connection to Mexico. The Texans of Mexican descent, known as *los Tejanos*, make up 55.6 percent of the population of San Antonio. They link the city's history to the history of the country just beyond its southern border. Furthermore, they have a deep sense of themselves as Texan. Cisneros admired "their sense of knowing they belong to the land, no matter what the textbooks say. The sense of belonging, of contributing to this history. Something I never felt in Illinois."[11]

She also enjoyed living where people "know how to pronounce your name. Where you can walk down the street and you're not the minority."[12] Cisneros found that listening to so much Spanish also fueled her writing with the rhythm of two languages and the variety of Spanish and English expressions that she drew into her stories. The Spanish was comforting and familiar to her, but Cisneros also enjoyed the way

Sandra Cisneros immediately felt at home in San Antonio, Texas. Here, children enjoy a local playground.

Texans spoke English, like her people, with a Spanish accent. "Being in Texas and listening to how people speak in Texas brought me back to my original love, and that is the rhythm of the spoken word," she said.[13]

The land as well as the people inspired Cisneros and fed her writing. She learned even more about San Antonio and the surrounding countryside when she received the 1985 Dobie-Paisano Fellowship, which paid her a small stipend and gave her living accommodations on a ranch for six months. The combination of so much open space and the blended cultures of Texas and Mexico greatly appealed to Cisneros:

> A landscape that matches the one inside me, one foot in this country, one in that. Graceful two-step, howl of an accordion, little gem and jewel, a little sad, a little joyous, that has made me whole. A place where two languages coexist, two cultures side by side. Not simply on street signs and condominiums. Not simply on menus and bags of corn chips. But in the public and private, sacred and profane, common and extraordinary circumstances of that homeland called the heart.[14]

Although she grew up in a much larger city in a completely different climate, she had found her home in San Antonio. "Because believe it or not, I'm home," Cisneros says. "Closer than I've ever been."[15]

Having found a place to call home and having found some measure of success, Sandra Cisneros did not want to leave San Antonio. She also did not want to leave the relative ease of being supported by funds from arts awards and grants given to her for published work and writing in progress. But unfortunately, she would be forced to do just that.

Ghosts and Voices

In the mid-1980s, Sandra Cisneros had found her home in San Antonio and success with *The House on Mango Street*. The years that followed, however, threw her back into the struggle to find enough time to write and enough income to support herself. From 1987 to 1989, Cisneros faced many challenges, both from the lack of outside financial support for her writing and from the abundance of her own inner "ghosts and voices."

The popularity of *The House on Mango Street* boosted the book into its third printing by 1987.

Cisneros found herself receiving fan mail and having people "get shy when they find out I'm me."[1] The fame from the book and all the elementary and college classes she visited was "rather incredible and wonderful," according to Cisneros. "I'm still not famous enough to make an American Express commercial and maybe I'll never be, but I'm the kind of famous that when I go into a local supermarket or shoe store some young child or college student will ask, 'Didn't you visit my class?'"[2]

But fame does not pay the bills, and by early 1987, the Dobie-Paisano Fellowship and other grant money ran out. Cisneros found herself posting flyers in local supermarkets and Laundromats for unsuccessful creative writing classes, desperate to find a way to stay in San Antonio. After having her waiter boyfriend support her for months, she felt she had no other choice but to leave her newly adopted home to accept a guest lectureship at California State University in Chico, California.

Leaving San Antonio was heart-wrenching for Cisneros, and she became increasingly depressed. However, the teaching position at Cal State, invigorating and challenging, gave her an adequate income, though it left her little time to write. She felt torn between the need to write and the urge to give her students all her energy. While many professors both write and teach writing, Cisneros found the two contradictory. She told her students that teaching and writing do not mix. She often found that when she wrote all weekend instead of reading her students' stories, she felt she was stealing their time.[3] When she put in all the necessary time to teach well, however, "my private time gets stolen because I can't write. My creativity is going towards them and to my teaching and to my one-on-one with them. I never find a balance."[4]

Furthermore, the university environment did not easily allow the kind of teaching she believed nurtured and strengthened young writers; teaching that emphasized learning how to write from one's own life experiences. The bell ringing at the end of each class, regardless of whether someone was in the middle of a sentence, was countercreative, says Cisneros. In addition, having to be in a certain place at a certain time was a challenge both for Cisneros, who habitually arrived late, and for her students, who were used to more punctual instructors. The inflexibility of classes ending at a specific time no matter what anyone was saying or doing did not make sense to Cisneros. "And I want to go out and drink with all of them, and have some coffee or beer after class, because I think the real learning keeps going."[5]

The real learning also kept going for Cisneros, caught between teaching and writing and between living in her beloved new home and the city of her employment. All the favorable reviews of her first book

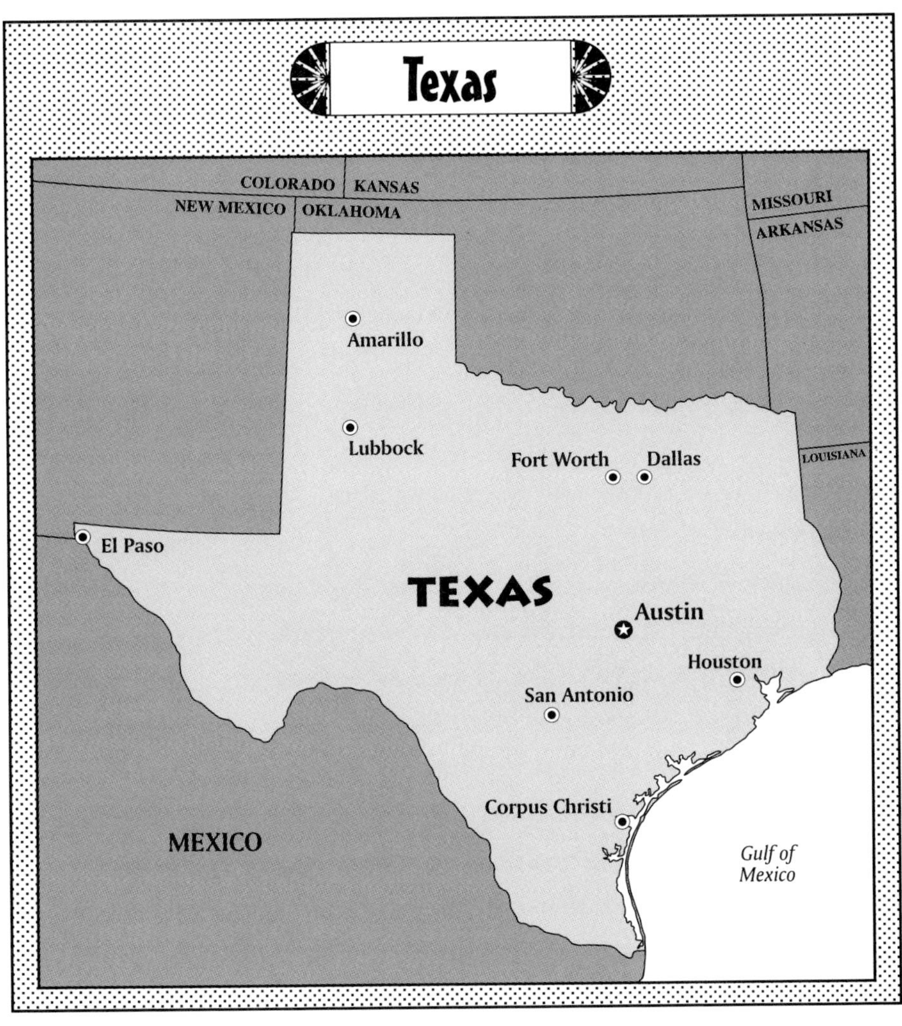

Sandra Cisneros enjoys the combination of American and Mexican cultures in San Antonio, Texas.

and all the awards had not made it any easier to make a living as a writer, and she did not see any hope for the situation changing. Eventually, Cisneros felt overtaken by depression. After finishing the poems to be published later that year as *My Wicked, Wicked Ways*, she felt trapped and stuck.

Her confidence was so shaken that she felt she could not teach or write. She would not even see Susan Bergholz, a literary agent who spent four years trying to find Cisneros to help her publish a second book of stories. Cisneros explains, "I thought I couldn't teach. I found myself becoming suicidal."[6] A friend of Cisneros's gave her Bergholz's phone number, but for months Cisneros did not call. "It was frightening because it was such a calm depression."[7] Her mental state made it hard for her to write or to believe in her writing enough to take action on its behalf.

Eventually, she worked her way out of her depression and mental blocks. First, she received a second National Endowment for the Arts fellowship in fiction, which "helped her get on her feet again, both financially and spiritually."[8] Then, she got up the nerve to dial Susan Bergholz's Manhattan phone number.

The call led to Cisneros's sending Bergholz a small selection of new stories. A few months later, Bergholz, with only thirty-nine pages in hand, sold *Woman Hollering Creek* to Joni Evans and Erroll McDonald at Random House/Vintage. Sandra Cisneros received a check for the largest advance ever given to a Chicano writer, one hundred thousand dollars.

Ten years after graduating from the University of Iowa Writers' Workshop, Sandra Cisneros finally found a way to make enough money from writing to "pay for my used car! Ha, ha! This is the first year that I'm not poor."[9] After years of turning down jobs that did not allow her enough time to write—sacrificing financial stability for her art—she now had enough money to live as a writer for some years to come. And she could return to San Antonio.

While she was writing the new book of fiction, her first full-length book of poetry was published by a small press, Third Woman Press, which specialized in the writings of women of color. *My Wicked Wicked Ways*, poems she had written since 1978, took its title from Cisneros's master's thesis for the University of Iowa Writers' Workshop in 1978. The title stayed, according to Cisneros, because, "these are the poems in which I write about myself, not a man writing about me." She believes that women who often define themselves according to their own terms are considered bad, evil, or just downright wicked. "And that's where I see perhaps the 'Wicked Wicked' of the title."[10] Yet to her surprise, the most controversial thing about *My Wicked, Wicked Ways* was not the way she wrote about her independence; it was the cover photo.

For the photo, Cisneros dressed in a slinky dress and cowboy boots, painted her lips bright red, and sat cross-legged with a cigarette in one hand and a glass of wine nearby. The cover, according to Cisneros, was both an homage to and a parody of black-and-white film stars like Rita Hayworth. Those "beautiful and cruel" women were famous when Cisneros was growing up. "They were the ones in control, and that was the only kind of role model I had for power," she explained in an interview.[11]

Although the reviews of the poetry were favorable, some people objected to the photo, thinking Cisneros wanted to be "beautiful and cruel." Cisneros explains that she purposely painted her lips bright red to show people she was joking. "I'm wearing cowboy boots!" she exclaims, "It's a fun photo."[12] Still, some found it offensive. "I'm surprised that some feminists said: 'How could you, a feminist, pose like lewd cheesecake to sell your book?,'" Cisneros adds.[13]

At first Cisneros was offended, but after thinking about it for a while, she marveled at people's lack of a sense of humor. "And why can't a feminist be sexy? Sexiness, I think, [is] a great feeling of self-empowerment."[14] Even if the book's front cover offended some, it empowered Cisneros and many women like her who could see the humor and truth in her cover photo as well as in her poetry.

The poems featured colorful images and stories about sex and love. In "I understand it as a kiss," she described the difference between her view and a boyfriend's view of love. Yet in other poems, she uses deadpan humor to put her views on love into perspective. In one poem, she wrote,

> I've learned two things.
> To let go
> clean as kite string.
> And to never wash a man's clothes.
> These are my rules.[15]

The idea of a Mexican-American woman making her own rules and following her own heart flew in the face of convention, explains Cisneros.

And one of the main themes of *My Wicked, Wicked Ways* traveled with Cisneros into *Woman Hollering Creek*: The theme of "redefining myself or controlling my own destiny or my own sexuality," explains Cisneros.[16] The difficulty of growing up under the rule of "seven fathers" as well as growing up both Catholic and Mexican made it difficult for Cisneros to take charge of her destiny at times. She describes that difficulty, along with all the other conflicts inside her, as ghosts. "So it's a ghost I'm still wrestling with," she explains.[17]

These ghosts both haunted and inspired her writing, but she discovered writing did not necessarily make the ghosts go away. "I used to think that writing was a way to exorcise those ghosts that inhabit the house that is ourselves," she explains. "But now I understand that only the little ghosts leave. The big ghosts still live inside you."[18] By writing stories and poems, she found she could make peace with her ghosts. "I think that it's a big step to be able to say: 'Well, yeah, I'm haunted, ha! There's a little ghost there and we coexist.'"[19]

The ghosts and voices (also the title of an essay by Cisneros) of the past, Cisneros explains, led her to write out of obsession, out of the need to make peace with the conflicts within her. She also came to believe that these ghosts and voices pushed many women of color to write not out of inspiration, but out of obsession, a need to express their worlds and themselves. She explains: "Perhaps later there will be time to write by inspiration. In the meantime, in my writing as well as in that of other Chicanas and other women, there is the necessary phase of dealing with those ghosts and voices most urgently haunting us, day by day."[20]

Nobody's Wife, Nobody's Mother

With the success of her new book *Woman Hollering Creek* and the opportunities that sprang from its success, Sandra Cisneros found herself well on the way to becoming a self-supporting writer with ample time to write. But she believed such success was only possible by being "nobody's wife, nobody's mother."[1] Without children or a husband, Cisneros was able to turn most of her attention toward her writing.

For Cisneros to place writing at the center of her life meant sacrificing time with boyfriends. After being involved with several boyfriends over the years, she realized that such relationships stole time from her writing. She explains that when she is deeply involved with a man, "he becomes my project."[2] Such a situation separates her from her writing and makes her angry with herself.

Even more difficult was explaining to concerned relatives why she was past thirty and still unmarried. In her poem "Old Maids," she write about her cousins and herself, all aunts and all unmarried. At weddings, family members used to ask Cisneros when she was getting married, but now, she says, they asked: "What happened in your childhood? Who hurt you? Who did this to you?" Cisneros wanted to answer, "Look, at your own marriage, tia [aunt], look at your marriage, mother, look at your marriage, abuela [grandmother], look at your marriages, tio [uncle], papa."[3] Cisneros claims she has never seen a woman in a marriage as happy as herself in her state of living alone.

While having a child appealed to Cisneros, she would have preferred that someone else be the principal caretaker of the child. "I would like to have a wife, instead of a husband, because then he could take care of the kids," she said.[4] Many of her male writer friends seemed to get a lot of work done, she explained, because they have wives. But if she married a man, she would have to devote most of her time and energy to her husband and children.

Her female writer friends with a husband and children faced many obstacles, explains Cisneros. "They get up very early in the morning, [get to] sleep very late at night; it's exhausting!, and they are writing at a much slower pace than they ought to be."[5] As nobody's wife, nobody's mother, especially with grants to support her, she was able to devote herself fully to her writing and give herself enough time doing other things to refuel herself. "My writing is my child and I don't want anything to come between us," Cisneros explains. Her private time allows her to replenish herself so she can write. "Sometimes all I want to do is turn the music on, walk around the house, dance by myself, do somersaults, and I don't want someone looking at me doing that," explains Cisneros. And when she is ready to write again, she needs ample time to read what she is writing aloud. "Or I need to cry or I want to laugh aloud and I don't want to explain why I'm laughing or why I'm crying."[6]

Probably at no other time had she been so immersed in either laughing or crying aloud as when she finished the manuscript of *Woman Hollering Creek*. The hefty advance and tight deadline forced her to discipline herself as a writer more than ever. "There's nothing like a deadline to teach you discipline, especially when you've already spent your advance," Cisneros says.[7] She soon found fear motivating her to write up to twelve hours a day.

Sandra Cisneros's Mexican heritage has had a profound effect on her writing.

Jim Sagel, who interviewed Cisneros in early 1991 for *Publishers Weekly*, said that she taped to her computer a prayer card to St. Jude, which she received from a Mexico City cabdriver. She would also light candles and read a bit each night before sitting down to write for hours, immersing herself so deeply in her stories that she heard the dialogue in her dreams. But the experience of being under the gun also empowered Cisneros: "Before, I'd be scratching my *nalgas* [behind], waiting for inspiration," she said. "Now I know I can work this hard. I know I did the best I could."[8]

The stories of *Woman Hollering Creek* give readers a glimpse into the lives of women who live day to day with the "triple bind of not being considered Mexican, not being considered American, and not being male."[9] Cisneros was determined to write stories that have not been written already, to "chart those barrio ditches and borderland arroyos [streams or brooks] that have not appeared on most copies of the American literary map but which, nonetheless, also flower into the 'mainstream,'" explained Jim Sagel. Achieving this feat allowed her to bridge the gap between the white and Latino worlds.

What she focused on most were the conditions of girls and women in the Latino community, including preteens, new brides, and women of great faith as well as deeply cynical women. According to an article in *Newsweek* magazine, the women in these stories ". . . are without exception strong girls, strong women."[10] The result is "a kind of choral work in which the harmonic voices emphasize the commonality of experience."[11] Cisneros herself says that while each story stands on its own, there is a "single, unifying thread of vision and experience that runs throughout the collection,"[12] the thread of strong women in *Woman Hollering Creek*.

Her editor, Julie Grau, says this book is not the work of a young writer but of a grown woman who draws on a "range of voice . . . to capture the extraordinary. This is the work of a poet." Sheila Benson of the *Los Angeles Times* adds, "Or a securely grounded woman, hollering in ringing tones, for all the world to hear."[13]

Not everyone took delight in the collection. Cisneros tells the story of another Latino writer who, on reading one of Cisneros's stories published in the *Los Angeles Times*, wrote a protest letter to the editor. He took offense with her portrayal of Mexican Americans and went on to accuse Cisneros and others who can attend "fancy workshops" of belittling their people. "But it is through the sweat and blood [of the Mexican people] that I've gone to school and benefited from all the labors of these people and now I'm writing about them," Cisneros explained.[14] What she did agree with, however, was that he had a right to protest because the *Los Angeles Times* had not published other representations of Mexicans.

Cisneros's representations brought her a great deal of glory. In 1991, she won the prestigious Lannan Literary Award for Fiction, a fifty-thousand-dollar prize given by the Lannan Foundation for the best book published that year. She also received a one-hundred-thousand-dollar advance from Turtle Bay Books for a new book, which was published in 1994 as *Loose*

Woman. Turtle Bay Books, a small press, also agreed to reissue *My Wicked, Wicked Ways*, since Third Woman Press had gone out of business. And the reprinting of fifteen thousand copies of *The House on Mango Street* propelled Cisneros on a ten-city book-signing tour in the spring of 1991. In addition, Chameleon Productions adapted the book into a play, which was performed the following year.

The constant traveling kept Cisneros from getting enough sleep or time to write. This occurred especially at colleges and universities where she would visit for a week or longer as an artist-in-residence. She spent time at the University of New Mexico in Albuquerque, the University of Michigan at Ann Arbor, the University of California at both Irvine and Berkeley, and at many other colleges and universities. At colleges, she would give well-attended readings, work with students in creative writing workshops, and discuss the writing life with faculty and students.

This success enabled Cisneros to finally establish herself in San Antonio. In 1991, Cisneros bought her first house, a Victorian home in King Williams, a historic area near old San Antonio. And to go with the old, she bought something new: a red pickup truck, complete with colorful Mexican fabric on the seats and ball fringe hanging from the inside of the windshield. She said it was the purchase of the truck, bought with money from her work, that most convinced her father that "telling stories was serious business."[15]

It was also a time that her father started to see the importance of her career choice beyond earning her money. She recalls going home at Christmas one year to find the usual "hot tamales and sweet tamales hissing in my mother's pressure cooker—and everybody—my mother, six brothers, wives, babies, aunts, cousins—talking too loud and at the same time, like in a Fellini film because that's just how we are."[16] She went upstairs to her father's room where he was recovering from a stroke he had had two years earlier, to find him watching a movie featuring Pedro Infante, a famed Mexican actor, and eating rice pudding. She handed him one of her stories translated into Spanish, and he soon punched the mute button on his remote control to read the story. She was delighted to hear him laugh at all the right places and read lines he liked out loud. He asked Cisneros if certain characters were people he knew. After years of her father making it clear to her that her role was to marry and have children, he surprised her. "When he was finally finished [reading], after what seemed like hours, my father looked up and asked, 'Where can we get more copies of this for the relatives?'"[17]

The recognition of thousands of strangers did not mean as much as the recognition from her father that she was a writer and that writing is a worthy occupation.

That recognition continued to enhance her sense of responsibility to those like her father, who had stories to tell, but could not or did not have opportunities to tell them.

In late 1992, Cisneros joined other Latino writers, including Mexican writers Rudolfo Anaya and Carlos Cumpian, on a journey south to introduce their work to Mexican and other Latin American readers and publishers. At the 1992 Feria Internacional del Libro (International Festival of Books) in Guadalajara, Mexico, she participated in panel discussions and readings. Cisneros also asked the publishers present why she was one of the only Chicana women writers in the world able to make a living from her work. Meanwhile, Mexican writers made their way north to participate in readings and discussions in the United States.

Cisneros addressed more than publishers, however. Speaking to nearly six hundred high school seniors in Los Angeles, who crammed onto gym bleachers to hear her, ". . . [she's] arrived as a star, no longer one of the 'illegal aliens of American lit' but a writer on the brink of mainstream literary recognition, with the full machinery of Random House behind her."[18] For Random House, as of 1991, published *Woman Hollering Creek* and bought rights to reprint *The House on Mango Street*.

After Cisneros read her story about Carmen, a heroine of "A Texas Operetta" who works for a San

Sandra Cisneros is an entertaining and inspirational lecturer.

Antonio law firm, she addressed a multicultural audience comprising Latinos, whites, Asian Americans, and African Americans. She implored them to remember their people. "You know something's growing up in your communities that heads of state are never going to see," she said. "And once you've seen it, you can't un-know it: Who's serving you. Who's washing the dishes. Who's sweeping the halls. What you know at a very early age gives you empathy and compassion."[19]

The empathy and compassion come from seeing people in pain, people without money, people without opportunities. The hope comes from seeing these people, "your communities," still serving and washing and sweeping, still find ways to keep themselves and those around them alive. And the writer, according to Cisneros, has an obligation to "Use what you know to help heal the pain in your community."[20]

As she acquired some power, she began to use it to the advantage of her people. In 1992, she refused to pose for an advertisement for Gap clothing stores, something that would have brought her a heavy dose of fame. The photograph was to be taken by the acclaimed Annie Leibovitz, a famous photographer of movie stars and musicians. Cisneros, after thinking about the offer, decided that the Gap was not doing enough for Latinos. "I'm in the position right now where I can afford to say, 'No, unless you do this,'" she said a year later. Still, it was not easy for an ugly duckling who grew up to be a famous swan to take a stand. "A part of me would like to go have my picture in a magazine because I was an ugly kid. But that's me personally," she says. "I'm no longer a person, I'm this collective. That's what's happened. It's not out of choice; it's out of circumstance."[21]

Being one of the few Latino writers in the country able to make a living from her writing also allowed her to help other writers. In 1993, when a bookstore owner in north Texas invited Cisneros to come to his store for a reading, she discovered he had never invited any other Latino writers in the past. She refused to go unless he asked other Latino writers to join her. She said it was important that Latino writers not only write their own stories but find ways to share those stories with the larger community.

Cisneros also took a stand on politics beyond the United States and Mexico. In January 1993, her friend from Sarajevo, Jasna, sent her a letter about the conditions of life in the city during the war. The Bosnian war, pitting Muslims against Serbs against Croats, had ripped many sections of the country apart, and Sarajevo, in particular, was heavily bombed and without needed services or resources for years. Jasna described the fear of living where one might be killed at any time as well as the difficulty of making do without running water or enough food and fuel. She wrote to Cisneros:

> I haven't taken a proper bath for months. We haven't had a single proper normal meal since the beginning of the war. We have almost no heating in the the houses, and nothing at all in our offices, schools, hospital. People are dying of cold. All the trees from the streets and city parks are gone. People have cut them in their struggle to survive, so Sarajevo may as well be called a city of fallen trees, a city of cemeteries, a city of grief and pain.[22]

Cisneros was so distraught by the letter that she used her clout to make a statement: She sent the letter to all the major newspapers in America, and in early April, it was printed on editorial pages from Atlanta to Los Angeles.

A few months later, Cisneros spoke out even more vehemently. At the International Women's Day Rally in San Antonio, she gave a speech, reprinted in newspapers across the country, begging for United States intervention to assist Sarajevo. Cisneros did not know who could solve the problems in Bosnia, but she demanded that someone do something. "Dear to Whom It May Concern, I've had it with the lot of you, all of you," she said. "A woman is there. . . . Get her out, I tell you. Get them out. They're in that city, that country, that region, that mouth of hell, that house on fire."[23] She went on to say that this woman was her friend and her sister, and that this somebody was crying out for help: "And I *hear* that somebody. And I *know* that somebody. . . . And I don't know what to do. I don't know what to do," Cisneros said.[24] Although she did not know what to do, she held weekly peace vigils for her friend through 1996 when Sarajevo finally escaped the nets of war.

Sandra Cisneros's efforts alerted more and more people to the horrors of a war far away. She helped Jasna tell the story of what it means to live, day by day, for years, in an unlivable situation. Cisneros may have been nobody's wife and nobody's mother, but she was somebody's friend for life, and in the Latino community, she was everybody's storyteller.

That House in the Heart

Sandra Cisneros has seen even greater success in the mid-1990s. Her books have found their way into classrooms, bookstores, libraries, and most of all, homes. In recent years, Spanish versions of several of her books have been published, making her writing available to a larger audience of Latinos. But more important, Cisneros discovered the riches of straddling two countries that have enhanced her life and especially her writing.

Cisneros's yearning to write and read aloud her stories and poems fortunately coincided with a Latino boom in the publishing world. Writers such as Jimmy Santiago Baca, Gary Soto, Julia Alvarez, Isabel Allende, and Laura Esquivel were suddenly more popular than ever in the 1990s. Laura Esquivel's *Like Water for Chocolate* has sold more than one hundred seventy thousand copies since 1983, and it was adapted into a popular movie. But it was more than movies that sold so many books by Latino writers. Several factors have created this boom, especially the increasing Latino population and the growth of magazines and publishers catering to the Latino market. There is also a growing hunger among Latinos to hear their stories told by their own people.

Publishers Weekly declared that the 1990s was a transition for Latino writers, from only being published by small presses with small press runs (number of books printed) to now being published by major publishing houses with press runs in the tens of thousands. This transition period was similar to that experienced by African-American writers such as Toni Morrison and Alice Walker in the 1970s, and experienced by Jewish writers such as Saul Bellow and Bernard Malamud in the 1950s.[1]

For Cisneros, the boom in Latino publishing has brought to her attention many writers who continue to influence her work. She has found the work of Latino writers Manuel Ruig, Juan Rulfo, Merce Rodereda, Ana Castillo, Tomas Rivera, and Denise Chavez particularly valuable. "There's a lot of good writing in the mainstream press that has nothing to say," explains Cisneros. "Chicano writers have a lot to say. The influence of our two languages is profound. The Spanish language is going to contribute something very rich to American literature."[2]

This transition period translated into larger publishers for Sandra Cisneros, too. In 1994, she had three books of her writing published. Vintage Books of Random House (one of the largest publishers in the United States) bought the rights to reprint *The House on Mango Street* from Arte Publico. In addition, Random House brought out *La Casa En Mango*, Elena Poniatowska's Spanish translation of *The House on Mango Street*. Knopf, another division of Random House, printed *Hairs/Pelitos*, a Spanish and English story for four- to eight-year-olds. Terry Ybanez illustrated "Hairs," one of the stories from *The House on Mango Street*, for children.

Because Cisneros wanted to continue supporting smaller presses, which are more apt to publish unknown writers and writers of color like herself, she would continue to publish her poetry with Turtle Bay Books. Fortunately, both Turtle Bay Books and Random House were able to pay her large advances and spend adequate money promoting all her books.

All the publishing activity, especially of so many Spanish versions of her writing, made Cisneros reflect more on how she blended Spanish and English in her writing. "I'm a translator," she said in 1993. "I'm an amphibian. I can travel in both worlds. What I'm saying is very important for the Latino community, but it is also important for the white community to hear. What I'm saying in my writing is that we can be Latino and still be American."[3] By drawing from both her languages, she discovered the best way to express her culture, one that would be shortchanged by using only English or only Spanish.

Although Cisneros speaks Spanish fluently, she rejects the idea of writing in Spanish or even translating her own mostly English books into Spanish. She says that she does not have the palette (range of expressions) in Spanish that she has in English. To get that range, one must be completely immersed in a Spanish-speaking country, Cisneros explained. "It's on the loaf of bread that you buy, it's on the radio jingle, it's on the graffiti you see, it's on your ticket stub. It must be all encompassing."[4]

By mixing the languages, however, Cisneros is able to draw from two cultures in expressing her people. The rhythm of Spanish and the sounds of English make a rich combination. "All of expresiones [expressions] in Spanish when translated make English wonderful," she said, giving the example of "exquisitas tacos," as one wonderful expression.[5] Cisneros enjoys the opportunity her storytelling and her poetry give her to "play" in the territory of two languages.

She went right in there to play in her 1994 collection of poems, *Loose Woman*. Reviewed favorably by many newspapers and magazines, the poetry of *Loose Woman* focuses on being a woman, both in love and in pain. Cisneros directs all the poems here from her heart, titling the three sections of the book "Little Clown, My heart," "The Heart Rounds Up the Usual Suspects," and "Heart, My Lovely Hobo." In writing these poems, she brought forth her usual wit and longing, her usual laments about the difficulties of being in love or alone. In "I Don't Like Being in Love," Cisneros writes about how being thirty-six or sixteen does not make too much of a difference. Love still feels risky and awkward, especially when "you don't know where. / And worse—with whom?"[6] This push and pull of relationships allowed Cisneros to face fears and hopes, says Joy Harjo, the Creek poet Cisneros befriended sixteen years earlier in the University of Iowa Writers' Workshop. "These poems are firecrackers and tequila, with a little candlelight and lace linen."[7]

While Cisneros says *My Wicked, Wicked Ways* is "in essence my wanderings in the desert," *Loose Woman* is "more a celebration of that house in the heart."[8] *My Wicked, Wicked Ways* is more about her time searching the barren landscape of her life for love, but *Loose Woman* focuses more on finding herself, and her love for herself. While loose might seem a strange word to use in celebrating that house, Cisneros explains that she is redefining the word *loose* in these poems: "I really feel that I'm [on] the loose and I've cut free from a lot of things that anchored me."[9] Part of what she freed herself from was writing mostly about being broken-hearted, not believing in herself enough, and not feeling as if she truly belonged anywhere.

"These poems are not so much a self-discovery as they are a reaffirmation of the self," asserts Raul Nino of *Booklist*.[10] Part of that reaffirmation included honoring her friendships, especially her friendship with Jasna. The book, dedicated to Jasna, "as if our lives depended on it," because Jasna's story about being trapped in a war-torn country showed Cisneros how "our lives" often do depend upon telling the truth.

Part of telling that truth includes writing a poem to Jasna. "I Awake in the Middle of the Night and Wonder If You've Been Taken" discusses Cisneros's fear that "At any moment, the soldiers could arrive" as well as her hope that "At any given second, Sarajevo could surrender."[11] She laments that Jasna does not count and women like her, caught in the cross fire, are not counted as history. The poem ends on a note of despair, Cisneros feeling hopeless both as a writer and as a woman to do anything to save Jasna's life: "I'm a woman like you. / I don't count either."[12]

In the act of writing, however, she found a way to count by telling the truth as she experienced it. Barbara Hoffert said in her review of *Loose Woman* that Cisneros "might as well be addressing the act of writing itself, which clearly brings out the best in her, along with the passion she associates with her Mexican roots."[13] These poems also have a great deal to do with the process of writing, a process that, for Cisneros, entails loosening up and telling the truth. Even her fiction reflects some truth. "All fiction is non-fiction," she explains. "Every piece of fiction is based on something that really happened."[14]

Poetry, which Cisneros defines as "the art of telling the truth," focuses on the truth that you do not usually show anybody. She advises writers not to think about their audience too much because such thinking may cause them to censor their own writing. To create something lasting, a writer must write through all the layers of appearance to "get at the core of truth" without knowing what that core is, explains Cisneros. "You just have to keep writing and hope that you'll come upon something that shocks you. When you think: 'Oh my goodness, I didn't know I felt that!', that's where you stop. That's the little piece of gold that you've been looking for. That's a poem."[15] Mining herself for poetry and her community for stories helps Cisneros bring to the surface little gems of truth.

The experience of writing such stories and poems has enriched Cisneros in literal ways, too. In 1995, she received a MacArthur Fellowship, often labeled by the media as a "genius grant," given out by the MacArthur Foundation to people in all fields of arts and sciences who exhibit extraordinary talent and promise. The two-hundred-twenty-five-thousand dollar grant awarded to Cisneros had no strings attached. She could use the money however she saw fit. In addition to this large sum, she received large advances for her books, fees paid to her for public readings, and artist-in-residence fees paid to her for workshops she gave at universities and colleges. Cisneros was finally on solid financial ground.

But the ground still most important to her was the land in and around San Antonio. She joined Navajo poet Luci Tapahonso to discuss the significance of living in the southwest in *The Desert Is No Lady*, an hour-long film made in 1995. The film, which celebrated women artists and writers of the southwest, included interviews with Cisneros as well as her reading from her works.

Farther away from home, she was invited in 1996—along with Pulitzer prize–winning and longtime notable authors such as Toni Morrison, Saul Bellow, John Updike, and Joseph Heller—to read at the Salon du Livre in Paris, an international celebration of books. Cisneros's other international ventures included reading her poetry at the Colegio de Mexico in Mexico City as well as at a symposium on Chicano literature in Germany and over Swedish Educational radio. But wherever she traveled, she would always return home to her house in San Antonio, close to the Mexican border and even closer to good Mexican food and good company.

In the last few years she has been at work on a new novel, *Carmelito*, which deals with the clash of Mexicans and Mexican Americans. Based on her own life, the book features a large cast of characters who, with humor and tenderness, tell the story of growing up between worlds, or as Cisneros puts it, "that clash of being a child, where when you went to Mexico the grandmother would just get so angry because of your American barbaric ways."[16] The book, written in the aftermath of her father's death in the mid-1990s, also concerns father-daughter relationships.

Cisneros also has hopes of branching out to other types of writing. She told the *Chicago Tribune* in 1992 that she dreamed of writing a Chicana feminist "telenovela," or soap opera as it is known in English. Cisneros sees this as an opportunity to reach out to a diverse audience. While she has said she cannot tell which direction her poetry will lead her, she is also interested in expanding her writing to include essays. And of course, there are many more stories and poems along the way.

After more than twenty years of writing her people's stories, she has created a life that honors her strength and talent. She has found a home balanced between the two worlds of Mexico and America, and the languages of Spanish and English. And she has reached a level of financial stability that allows her to keep writing at the center of her life. Although she wrote of a "home in the heart" back in 1982, she now realizes the true meaning of that home:

> I've come this year to realize who I am, to feel very very strong and powerful, I am at peace with myself and I don't feel terrified by anyone, or by any terrible word that anyone would launch at me from either side of the border. I guess I've created a house made [of] bricks that no big bad wolf can blow down now.[17]

Sandra Cisneros has found peace with herself, a home where she feels she belongs, the means to make a living as a poet and fiction writer, and the opportunity to help others in the Latino community. As an activist and a writer, Cisneros tells the stories of the Latino community while fighting for more opportunities for her people.

Chronology

1954— Sandra Cisneros is born December 20 in Chicago.

1959— Cisneros begins public elementary school, later attending Catholic schools such as St. Callitus and St. Aloysius.

1966— Cisneros's parents buy their first house, a bungalow in the barrio on the 1500 block of N. Campbell Ave. in Chicago.

1968— Cisneros begins Josephium High School (Catholic all-girls school).

1972— After graduating from high school in the spring, Cisneros begins Loyola University in Chicago in the fall.

1976— Cisneros graduates from Loyola University in the spring and begins University of Iowa Writers' Workshop M.F.A. program in creative writing in the fall.

1978— Cisneros begins writing sketches for *The House on Mango Street*, finishes a master's thesis called "My Wicked, Wicked Ways," and receives M.F.A. from University of Iowa Writers' Workshop.

1979–81— Returning to Chicago, Cisneros works at Latino Youth Alternative High School, counseling students.

1980–81—Cisneros works as an administration assistant for Loyola University. Her first collection of poems (a chapbook), *Bad Boys*, is published in 1980.

1982—Receiving her first National Endowment of the Arts grant, Cisneros leaves Chicago for Massachusetts to finish *The House on Mango Street*.

1982–83—Cisneros travels throughout Europe, serving as resident poet at Michael Karolyi Artist's Foundation in Venice, Italy, and spending a summer in Sarajevo (Yugoslavia).

1984—*The House on Mango Street* is published by Arte Publico Press; Cisneros receives rave reviews. Cisneros serves as literary director of Guadalupe Cultural Arts Center of San Antonio, Texas.

1985—After receiving the Before Columbus American Book Award for *The House on Mango Street*, Cisneros is granted a Dobie-Paisano Fellowship.

1987—*My Wicked, Wicked Ways*, a collection of poems named after her master's thesis, is published by Third Woman Press, and Cisneros serves as a visiting professor at California State University at Chico. Later in the year she receives her second NEA grant, and she contacts Susan Bergholz, literary agent, who sells *Woman Hollering Creek* and *The House on Mango Street* to Random House and Vintage (a division of Random House).

1991— *Woman Hollering Creek* is published by Random House, and Cisneros receives the Lannan Literary Award. Vintage Books reprints *The House on Mango Street*.

1992— Cisneros receives a large advance from Random House for a novel, *Carmelito*, and another for a new collection of poetry, *Loose Woman*. Turtle Bay also reissues *My Wicked, Wicked Ways* in hardcover.

1993— The letter Cisneros receives from her friend in Sarajevo and Cisneros's response to the war in Sarajevo is printed in most major newspapers across the country.

1994— Random House publishes *Loose Woman*. Knopf publishes *Hairs/Pelitos* (a children's book).

1995— Cisneros receives a MacArthur Fellowship ("genius grant"). Random House publishes *La Casa en Mango Street* (Spanish version of *The House on Mango Street*), translated by Elena Poniatowska.

Sandra Cisneros's poems, stories, and essays have been published in *Texas Humanist*, *Tonantzin*, *Humanizarte*, *Third Woman*, *Americas Review*, *Glamour*, *The New York Times Book Review*, *Ms.*, and many other publications.

Selected Works by Sandra Cisneros

The House on Mango Street, 1984

My Wicked Wicked Ways, 1987

Woman Hollering Creek, 1991

Hairs: Pelitos, 1994

Loose Woman, 1994

La Casa en Mango Street (Spanish version), 1995

Chapter Notes

Chapter 1. The Girl With the Bad Report Cards

1. Mary B.W. Tabor, "A Solo Traveler in Two Worlds," *The New York Times*, January 7, 1993, p. C1.
2. Ibid.
3. Ibid.
4. Ibid.
5. Peter S. Prescott, with Karen Springen, "Seven for Summer," *Newsweek*, June 3, 1991, p. 60.
6. Susan Wood, "The Voice of Esperanza," *Washington Post Book Review*, June 9, 1991, p. 3.
7. Bebe Moore Campbell, "Crossing Borders," *The New York Times Book Review*, May 26, 1991, p. 8.
8. Tabor, p. C10.
9. Ibid.
10. Carlos Fuentes, "The Blending, and Clashing, of Cultures," *Christian Science Monitor*, June 1, 1992, p. 15.

Chapter 2. Straddling Two Countries

1. Feroza Jussawalla and Reed Way Dasenbrock, *Interviews With Writers of the Post-Colonial World* (Jackson: University Press of Mississippi, 1992), pp. 286–306.
2. Ibid., p. 297.
3. Ibid.
4. Ibid.
5. Sandra Cisneros, "Poem as Preface," *The New York Times Book Review*, September 6, 1992, p. 1.
6. Jussawalla and Dasenbrock, p. 296.
7. Adria Bernardi, "Latino Voice," *Chicago Tribune*, August 4, 1991, p. K6.
8. Sandra Cisneros, "Ghosts and Voices: Writing from Obsession," *The Americas Review*, vol. 15, no. 1, Spring 1987, p. 69.
9. Sheila Benson, "From the Barrio to the Brownstone," *Los Angeles Times*, May 7, 1991, p. F1.

10. Ibid.
11. Adria Bernardi, p. K6.
12. Sandra Cisneros, "Ghosts and Voices: Writing from Obsession," p. 69.
13. Benson, p. F1.
14. Jim Sagel, "Sandra Cisneros," *Publishers Weekly*, March 29, 1991, p. 74.
15. Pilar E. Rodriguez Aranda, "On the Solitary Fate of Being Mexican, Female, Wicked, and Thirty-three: An Interview With Sandra Cisneros," *The Americas Review*, vol. 19, no. 1, Spring 1990, p. 66.
16. Cisneros, "Ghosts and Voices," p. 69.
17. Ibid.
18. Sagel, p. 74.
19. Aranda, p. 66.

Chapter 3. Seven Fathers and One Strong-Willed Mother

1. Sandra Cisneros, "Only Daughter," *Glamour*, November 1990, p. 256.
2. Pilar E. Rodriguez Aranda, "On the Solitary Fate of Being Mexican, Female, Wicked, and Thirty-three: An Interview With Sandra Cisneros," *The Americas Review*, vol. 19, no. 1, p. 68.
3. Ibid.
4. Ibid., p. 73.
5. Sandra Cisneros, "Ghosts and Voices: Writing from Obsession," *The Americas Review*, vol. 15, no. 1, Spring 1987, p. 69.
6. Cisneros, "Only Daughter," p. 256.
7. Ibid.
8. Ibid.
9. Aranda, p. 79.
10. Ibid.
11. Raul Nino, "The Booklist Interview: Sandra Cisneros," *Booklist*, vol. 90, September 1993, p. 36.
12. Andrew Chavez, "Sandra Cisneros," in *Notable Hispanic American Women*, ed. Diane Telgen and Jim Kamp (Detroit: Gale Research, Inc., 1993), p. 99.
13. Jim Sagel, "Sandra Cisneros," *Publishers Weekly*, March 29, 1991, p. 74.
14. Sandra Cisneros, "Guadalupe: The Sex Goddess," *Ms.*, July–August 1996, p. 44.
15. "Sandra Cisneros: Giving Back to the Libraries," *Schools Journal*, vol. 119, no. 1, January 1992, p. 55.

16. Cisneros, "Ghosts and Voices," p. 69.
17. Ibid., p. 71.
18. Ibid.
19. Ibid.
20. Sandra Cisneros, "Notes to a Young(er) Writer," *The Americas Review*, vol. 15, no. 1, Spring 1987, p. 74.
21. Cisneros, "Ghosts and Voices," p. 69.
22. Cisneros, "Guadalupe the Sex Goddess," p. 44.
23. Cisneros, "Notes to a Young(er) Writer," p. 74.
24. Ibid.
25. Ibid., p. 76.
26. Aranda, p. 66.

Chapter 4. A Yellow Weed Among the Hothouse Flowers

1. Sandra Cisneros, "Only Daughter," *Glamour*, November 1990, p. 256.
2. Ibid.
3. Eduardo F. Elias, "Sandra Cisneros," *Dictionary of Literary Biography*, vol. 122, ed. Karen Rood (Detroit: Gale Research Inc., 1992), p. 78.
4. "Sandra Cisneros," in *Great Women Writers*, ed. Frank N. Magill (New York: Henry Holt, 1994), p. 102.
5. Elias, p. 78.
6. *Authors and Artists for Young Adults*, quoted in Andres Chavez, "Sandra Cisneros," *Notable Hispanic American Women*, ed. Diane Telgen and Jim Kamp (Detroit: Gale Research, Inc., 1993), p. 10.
7. Feroza Jussawalla and Reed Way Dasenbrock, *Interviews With Writers of the Post-Colonial World* (Jackson: University Press of Mississippi, 1992), p. 302.
8. Ibid.
9. Jim Sagel, "Sandra Cisneros," *Publishers Weekly*, March 29, 1991, p. 74.
10. Ibid.
11. Pilar E. Rodriguez Aranda, "On the Solitary Fate of Being Mexican, Female, Wicked, and Thirty-three: An Interview With Sandra Cisneros," *The Americas Review*, vol. 19, no. 1, Spring 1990, p. 65.
12. Ibid.
13. Ibid.
14. Sandra Cisneros, "Ghosts and Voices: Writing from Obsession," *The Americas Review*, vol. 15, no. 1, Spring 1987, p. 70.

15. Ibid.

Chapter 5. Back to the Barrio

1. Sandra Cisneros, "Ghosts and Voices: Writing from Obsession," *The Americas Review*, vol. 15, no. 1, Spring 1987, p. 71.

2. Ibid.

3. Feroza Jassawalla and Reed Way Dasenbrock, *Interviews With Writers of the Post-Colonial World* (Jackson: University Press of Mississippi, 1992), p. 291.

4. Cisneros, "Ghosts and Voices: Writing from Obsession," p. 70.

5. Sandra Cisneros, "Do You Know Me?: I Wrote *The House on Mango Street*," *The Americas Review*, vol. 15, no. 1, Spring 1987, p. 77.

6. Ibid.

7. Jussawalla and Dasenbrock, p. 298.

8. Pilar E. Rodriguez Aranda, "On the Solitary Fate of Being Mexican, Female, Wicked and Thirty-three: An Interview With Sandra Cisneros," *The Americas Review*, vol. 19, no. 1, Spring 1990, p. 69.

9. Ibid.

10. Ibid.

11. Sandra Cisneros, *The House on Mango Street* (Houston: Arte Publico, 1984), p. 10.

12. Mary B.W. Tabor, "A Solo Traveler in Two Worlds," *The New York Times Literary Review*, January 7, 1993, p. C10.

13. Cisneros, *The House on Mango Street*, p. 110.

Chapter 6. Borderland Blessings, Borderland Blues

1. Sandra Cisneros, "Do You Know Me?: I Wrote *The House on Mango Street*," *The Americas Review*, vol. 15, no. 1, Spring 1987, p. 79.

2. Sandra Cisneros, "Who Wants Stories Now?" *The New York Times*, March 14, 1993, sec. 4, p. 17.

3. Ibid.

4. Ibid.

5. Ibid.

6. Ibid.

7. Feroza Jussawalla and Reed Way Dasenbrock, *Interviews With Writers of the Post-Colonial World* (Jackson: University Press of Mississippi, 1992), p. 298.

8. Raul Nino, "The Booklist Interview: Sandra Cisneros," *Booklist*, vol. 90, no. 1, September 1993, p. 36.

9. Jussawalla and Dasenbrock, p. 299.

10. Ibid.

11. Sandra Cisneros, "The Tejano Soul of San Antonio," *Texas Magazine*, May 17, 1992, p. 24.

12. Ibid.

13. Jussawalla and Dasenbrock, p. 291.

14. Ibid.

15. Ibid.

Chapter 7. Ghosts and Voices

1. Sandra Cisneros, "Do You Know Me?: I Wrote *The House on Mango Street*," *The Americas Review*, vol. 15, no. 1, Spring 1987, p. 77.

2. Ibid.

3. Pilar E. Rodriguez Aranda, "On the Solitary Fate of Being Mexican, Female, Wicked, and Thirty-three: An Interview With Sandra Cisneros," *The Americas Review*, vol. 18, no. 1, Spring 1990, p. 77.

4. Ibid.

5. Ibid., p. 78.

6. Jim Sagel, "Sandra Cisneros," *Publishers Weekly*, March 29, 1991, p. 74.

7. Ibid.

8. Ibid.

9. Aranda, p. 69.

10. Ibid., p. 67.

11. Ibid., p. 68.

12. Ibid.

13. Ibid., p. 69.

14. Ibid.

15. Sandra Cisneros, *My Wicked, Wicked Ways* (Bloomington, Ind.: Third Woman Press, 1987), p. 32.

16. Aranda, p. 67.

17. Ibid.

18. Ibid.

19. Ibid.

20. Sandra Cisneros, "Ghosts and Voices: Writing from Obsession," *The Americas Review*, vol. 15, no. 1, Spring 1987, p. 73.

Chapter 8. Nobody's Wife, Nobody's Mother

1. Sandra Cisneros, *The House on Mango Street* (New York: Random House, 1991).

2. Feroza Jussawalla and Reed Way Dasenbrock, *Interviews With Writers of the Post-Colonial World* (Jackson: University Press of Mississippi, 1992), p. 298.

3. Ibid.

4. Ibid.

5. Pilar E. Rodriguez Aranda, "On the Solitary Fate of Being Mexican, Female, Wicked, and Thirty-three: An Interview With Sandra Cisneros," *The Americas Review*, vol. 19, no. 1, Spring 1990, p. 67.

6. Ibid., p. 72.

7. Ibid., p. 73.

8. Jim Sagel, "Sandra Cisneros," *Publishers Weekly*, March 29, 1991, p. 74.

9. "Sandra Cisneros," *World Authors, 1985–1990*, ed. Vineta Colby (Bronx, N.Y.: H. W. Wilson, 1995), p. 146.

10. Peter S. Prescott with Karen Springen, "Seven for Summer," *Newsweek*, June 3, 1991, p. 60.

11. Eduardo F. Elias, "Sandra Cisneros," *Dictionary of Literary Biography*, vol. 122, ed. Karen Rood (Detroit: Gale Research, Inc., 1992), p. 79.

12. *World Authors*, p. 147.

13. Sheila Benson, "From the Barrio to the Brownstone," *Los Angeles Times*, May 7, 1991, p. F7.

14. Jussawalla and Dasenbrock, p. 294.

15. Rosemary L. Bray, "A Deluge of Voices," *The New York Times Book Review*, May 26, 1991, p. 6.

16. Sandra Cisneros, "Only Daughter," *Glamour*, November 1990, p. 256.

17. Ibid.

18. Benson, p. F7.

19. Ibid.

20. Ibid.

21. Carlos Fuentes, "The Blending, and Clashing, of Cultures," *Christian Science Monitor*, June 1, 1992, p. 19.

22. Jasna, "Letter from Sarajevo," *The New York Times*, April 9, 1993, p. A12.

23. Sandra Cisneros, "Who Wants Stories Now?" *The New York Times*, April 14, 1993, sec. 4, p. 17.

24. Ibid.

Chapter 9. That House in the Heart

1. Joseph Barbato, "Latino Writers in the American Market," *Publishers Weekly*, February 1, 1991, p. 18.

2. Jim Sagel, "Sandra Cisneros," *Publishers Weekly*, March 29, 1991, p. 75.

3. Mary B.W. Tabor, "A Solo Traveler in Two Worlds," *The New York Times Literary Review*, January 7, 1993, p. 6.

4. Pilar E. Rodriguez Aranda, "On the Solitary Fate of Being Mexican, Female, Wicked, and Thirty-three: An Interview With Sandra Cisneros," *The Americas Review*, vol. 19, no. 1, Spring 1990, p. 67.

5. Ibid.

6. Ibid.

7. Sandra Cisneros, *Loose Woman* (New York: Vintage/Random House, 1994), book note.

8. Aranda, p. 74.

9. Ibid., p. 79.

10. Raul Nino, *Booklist*, May 1, 1994, p. 1576.

11. Ibid., p. 64.

12. Ibid.

13. Barbara Hoffert, *Loose Woman: Poems* [book review], *Library Journal*, May 15, 1994, p. 76.

14. Aranda, p. 64.

15. Ibid.

16. Feroza Jussawalls and Reed Way Dasenbrock, *Interviews With Writers of the Post-Colonial World* (Jackson: University Press of Mississippi, 1992), p. 296.

17. Aranda, p. 74.

Further Reading

Chavez, Andres. "Sandra Cisneros." Notable Hispanic American Women. Edited by Diane Telgen and Jim Kamp, 99–101. Detroit: Gale Research, Inc., 1993.

Cisneros, Sandra. *The House on Mango Street*. New York: Random House, 1991. Originally published by Arte Publico, 1984.

———. "Ghosts and Voices: Writing from Obsession." *Americas Review*, vol. 15, no. 1, Spring 1987, 69–73.

———. "Notes to a Young(er) Writer." *Americas Review*, vol. 15, no. 1, Spring 1987, 74–76.

———. "Only Daughter." *Glamour*, November 1990, 256–258.

———. "Poem as Preface." *The New York Times Book Review*, September 6, 1992, 1.

———. "Who Wants Stories Now?" *The New York Times*, March 14, 1993, 4–17.

Elias, Eduardo F. "Sandra Cisneros." *Dictionary of Literary Biography*, vol. 122. Edited by Karen Rood, 77–81. Detroit: Gale Research, Inc., 1992.

Fuentes, Carlos. "The Blending, and Clashing, of Cultures." *Christian Science Monitor*, June 1, 1992, 15.

Moore Campbell, Bebe. "Crossing Borders." *The New York Times Book Review*, May 26, 1991, 6.

"Sandra Cisneros: Giving Back to Libraries." *Library Journal*, vol. 117, no. 1, January 1992, 55.

"Sandra Cisneros." *Great Women Writers*. Edited by Frank N. Magill, 102–105. New York: Henry Holt, 1994.

"Sandra Cisneros." *World Authors, 1985–1990*. Edited by Vineta Colby, 146–148. Bronx, N.Y.: H. W. Wilson, 1995.

Tabor, Mary B. W. "A Solo Traveler in Two Worlds." *The New York Times Literary Review*, January 7, 1993, 6–8.

INDEX